SOFTWARE LICENSE AGREEMENT

THANK YOU FOR LICENSING THE USE OF THE ACCOMPANYING SOFTWARE PRODUCT. IT IS IMPORTANT THAT YOU (THE "LICENSEE") READ THESE TERMS CAREFULLY. THESE ARE THE ONLY TERMS AND CONDITIONS APPLICABLE TO YOUR USE OF THE SOFTWARE PRODUCT. THE SOFTWARE PRODUCT IS PROTECTED BY COPYRIGHT LAWS AND INTERNATIONAL COPYRIGHT TREATIES, AS WELL AS OTHER INTELLECTUAL PROPERTY LAWS. ALL RIGHTS NOT EXPRESSLY GRANTED TO YOU IN THIS LICENSE AGREEMENT ARE RESERVED TO SERIF (EUROPE) LIMITED OR ITS LICENSORS. THE SOFTWARE PRODUCT IS LICENSED, NOT SOLD.

This Software License Agreement ("License Agreement") is a legal agreement between you (either an individual or a single entity) and Serif (Europe) Limited ("Serif") for the accompanying Software Product, which includes computer software and may include associated media, printed materials, and "online" or electronic documentation (all referred to as the "Software Product"). By installing, displaying, copying, accessing or otherwise using the Software Product, you, the Licensee, agree to be bound by the terms of this License Agreement. If you do not agree to the terms of this License Agreement, do not install display, access or use the Software Product and please return it to your place of purchase. If the Software Product is returned within 14 days of purchase with proof of purchase you will be offered a full refund of the price you paid.

1. GRANT OF LICENSE

Subject to the Licensee complying with these terms and in consideration of the Licensee's obligations and undertakings in this License Agreement Serif hereby grants to Licensee a personal, non-exclusive, non-transferable license to use one (1) copy of the Software Product, including any upgrades provided by Serif, according to these terms on a single computer.

2. SCOPE OF USE

Licensee may install, display, access and use one (1) copy of the Software Product on a single computer. The primary user of the computer on which the Software Product is installed may make a second copy of the computer software part of the Software Product for his or her exclusive use on a portable computer. Licensee may store or install one (1) copy of the Software Product on a storage device, such as a network server, only to install or run the Software Product on other computers over an internal network and subject to Licensee first acquiring and dedicating a license for each separate computer on which the Software Product is installed, displayed, accessed or used from the storage device. The Software Product may not be shared or used concurrently on different computers. One (1) copy of the computer software part of the Software Product may be made for back-up or archival purposes but that copy shall be used for no other purpose. If the Software Product is labelled "Not for Resale" or "NFR," Licensee's use of the Software Product is strictly limited to use for demonstration, test, or evaluation purposes only and no other use. The associated media, printed materials and "online" or electronic documentation shall not be copied and are for use only with the computer software part of the Software Product.

3. PROHIBITIONS

Licensee shall not:-

3.1 modify or alter the whole or any part of the Software Product nor merge any part of it with another software product nor separate any components of the Software Product from the Software Product nor, save to the extent and in the circumstances permitted by law, create derivative works from, or, reverse engineer, decompile, disassemble or otherwise derive source code from the Software Product or attempt to do any of these things

3.2 copy the Software Product (except as provided above)

3.3 assign rent, transfer, sell, disclose, deal in, make available or grant any rights in the Software Product in any form to any person without the prior written consent of Serif;

3.4 remove alter, obscure, interfere with or add to any proprietary notices, labels, trade marks, names or marks on, annexed to, or contained within the Software Product;

3.5 use the Software Product in any manner that infringes the intellectual property or other rights of Serif or any other party; or

3.6 use the Software Product to provide on-line or other database services to any other person.

4. INTELLECTUAL PROPERTY RIGHTS AND TERMINATION

Licensee acknowledges that:

4.1 all title to the copyright and all other intellectual property rights in and to the Software Product, its accompanying documentation and any copy made by Licensee are the exclusive property of and remain with Serif and/or its licensor(s),

4.2 the Software Product and all copies thereof are Serif's exclusive property and constitute confidential information and a valuable trade secret of Serif.

4.3 any unauthorized copying of the Software Product, or failure to comply with any of the provisions of this License Agreement (each, a "Terminable Event"), will result in automatic termination of this License Agreement and all licenses granted under this License Agreement and Licensee must destroy all copies of the Software Product. In the event of a breach of this License Agreement by Licensee, Serif reserves and shall have available all legal remedies.

5. CUSTOMER SPECIFIC VERSION

If the Software Product is a customer specific version or license ("Customer Specific Version") then the license to use the Software Product shall only be valid if the status of the Licensee at the time of purchase entitled them to be a valid licensee of the Customer Specific Version. Customer Specific Versions include but are not limited to Student, Teacher and OEM/Bundle Purchase versions and are identified on the media, packaging or within the software of the Software Product. If you are in any doubt as to whether your status at the time of purchase entitled you to be a valid licensee of a Customer Specific Version then please contact Serif customer service for further information.

6. LIMITED TERM OF LICENSE FOR TRIAL VERSION SOFTWARE

If the Software Product is a trial, locked, demonstration or other limited use version of the Software Product (all referred to as a "Trial Version") then the license to use the Software Product shall expire in accordance with the terms set out in such Trial Version. On the expiration of the license for the Trial Version, Licensee will be required to purchase a full license of the Software Product to continue use.

7. LIMITED WARRANTY AND DISCLAIMER

Serif warrants that for a period of thirty (30) days after delivery to Licensee the diskettes, CD-ROMs or DVD-ROMs on which the computer software included in the Software Product is supplied will, under normal use, be free from defects that prevent Licensee from loading the Software Product on to a computer. Serif's entire liability and Licensee's exclusive remedy under this warranty will be, at Serif's option, to (a) use reasonable commercial efforts to attempt to correct or work around errors, or (b) to replace the Software Product with a functionally equivalent Software Product, on a diskette, CD-ROM or DVD-ROM, as applicable or (c) return the price paid for the Software Product, in each case subject to Licensee having paid for the Software Product in full and upon return of the Software Product to Serif together with a copy of Licensee's receipt for its purchase. This Limited Warranty shall not apply if failure of the Software Product media has resulted from accident, abuse, misuse or misapplication. Any replacement Software Product will be warranted for the remainder of the original warranty period or thirty (30) days from delivery to Licensee, whichever is longer. Outside the United Kingdom, neither these remedies nor any product support services offered by Serif are available without proof of purchase from a distributor authorized by Serif. The Software Product is licensed on an "as is" basis without any warranty of any nature.

8. NO OTHER WARRANTIES

Except for the above express limited warranty, all warranties conditions, terms and duties either expressed or implied by law and relating to merchantability, quality, fitness and/or non-infringement with regard to the Software Product and the provision of or failure to provide support services are excluded to the fullest extent permitted by law. Licensee shall be solely responsible for the selection, use, efficiency and suitability of the Software Product and Serif shall have no liability therefor. Serif shall have no liability for, nor obligation to indemnify Licensee regarding actions alleging the infringement of proprietary rights by the Software Product. Serif does not warrant that the operation of the Software Product will be uninterrupted or error free or that the Software Product will meet Licensee's specific requirements. Nothing in this License Agreement shall exclude or limit any statutory rights which cannot be excluded or limited due to Licensee acting as a consumer. Any provisions which would be void under any legislation shall to that extent have no force or effect

9. LIMITATION OF LIABILITY

In no event will Serif or its suppliers be liable for loss and/or corruption of data, loss of profits, damage to goodwill, cost of cover, any pure economic, special, incidental, punitive, exemplary, consequential or indirect damages or losses and/or any business interruption, loss of business, loss of contracts, loss of opportunity and/or loss of production arising from or in connection with the use of the Software Product, however caused. Each limitation will apply even if Serif or its authorized distributor has been advised of the possibility of such damage and shall be deemed to be repeated and apply as a separate provision for each of liability in contract, tort, breach of a statutory duty, breach of common law and/or under any other legal basis. In no event will Serif's liability exceed the amount Licensee paid for the Software Product. Licensee acknowledges that these limitations are necessary to allow Serif to provide the Software Product at its current prices. If modification to these limitations is required Serif will agree appropriate amendment for payment of a higher than current price for the Software Product. Nothing in this License Agreement shall exclude or limit Serif's liability for death or personal injury due to its negligence or any liability due to its fraud or any other liability which may not be limited or excluded as a matter of law.

10. TERMINATION

Licensee may terminate this License Agreement at any time. Serif may terminate this License Agreement if Licensee fails to comply with the terms and conditions of this License Agreement. In either event all licenses granted under this Agreement shall end immediately and Licensee must destroy all copies of the Software Product. All terms which by their nature should survive termination of this License Agreement shall survive its termination.

11. UPGRADE and REPLACEMENTS

If the Software Product is being provided to Licensee as an upgrade to, physical copy of, or a replacement for (collectively known as "Replacement Software"), software which Licensee has been previously licensed from Serif (such software referred to as the "Prior Software"), then Licensee agrees to erase or destroy all copies of the Prior Software (except, if required, for one backup copy of the Prior Software) within thirty (30) days of first installing, displaying or accessing this Software Product. In order to install, display, access or otherwise use Replacement Software for Prior Software, Licensee must have a valid license for the related Prior Software for this License Agreement to be valid. Upon installing, accessing, displaying, or otherwise using the Replacement Software for the Prior Software (except for the one copy for back-up purpose only) all licenses of the Prior Software will cease immediately and this License Agreement replaces such license for the Prior Software. The total number of Replacement Software for Prior Software a Licensee may acquire may not exceed the total number of computers that were licensed by Licensee to run, display, access or otherwise utilize the Prior Software.

12. GUIDELINES FOR THE USE OF DIGITAL CONTENT AND INDEMNITY

The Software Product may contain templates, clipart, photo images, video and/or audio media files (collectively referred to as the "Digital Content") which are either owned by Serif or licensed to Serif from a third party. Subject to adhering to the terms of this License Agreement and to the restrictions in this clause unless expressly granted to Licensee all rights to the Digital Content are reserved to Serif and/or its licensors. Licensee is hereby licensed to use, modify, and publish the Digital Content upon the terms of this License Agreement. If Licensee is uncertain as to whether any intended use complies with these terms Licensee should seek the advice of an attorney or legal counsel.

A. LICENSEE MAY, subject to any restrictions set out below:

1. incorporate any Digital Content into Licensee's own original work and publish, display, and distribute that work in any media. Licensee may not sell, supply, resell, sublicense, or otherwise make available the Digital Content for use or distribution separately or detached from a product or Web page created by Licensee. For example, the Digital Content may be used as part of a Web page design, but may not be made available for downloading separately or in a format designed or intended for permanent storage or re-use by others. Licensee's, clients may be provided with copies of the Digital Content (including digital files) as an integral part of a work product created by Licensee, but may not be provided with the Digital Content or permitted to use the Digital Content separately or as part of any other product; Licensee may not sell, or otherwise distribute for compensation, money, money's worth or consideration of any kind, greeting cards created with the Software Product, which include the Digital Content.

2. make one (1) copy of the Digital Content for backup or archival purposes.

B. LICENSEE MAY NOT:

1. create scandalous, obscene, defamatory, or immoral works using the Digital Content nor use the Digital Content for any purpose prohibited by law;

2. use or permit the use of the Digital Content or any part thereof as a trademark or service mark, or claim any proprietary rights of any sort in the Digital Content or any part thereof;

3. use the Digital Content in electronic format, on-line, or in multimedia applications unless (a) the Digital Content is incorporated for viewing purposes only and (b) no permission is given to download and/or save the Digital Content for any reason;

4. rent, lease, sublicense, charge or lend the Digital Content, or a copy thereof, to another person or legal entity;

5. use any Digital Content except as expressly permitted by this License Agreement and without prejudice to any other right or remedy Serif may have Licensee indemnifies and shall keep indemnified Serif ,its licensors and authorised distributors against all and any claims actions, liability, costs, proceedings, awards, damages, losses, demands, expenses, fines, loss of profits, penalties, loss of reputation, judgements and any other liabilities including legal costs (without set-off counterclaim or reduction) suffered by Serif and/or its licensors and /or its authorised distributors arising out of or in connection with the use of the Software Product and/or use or distribution of the Digital Content by the Licensee and/or any of its clients whether or not such losses were foreseeable or foreseen at the date of this License Agreement.

C. MPEGLA, MPEG

Any use of this product other than consumer personal use in any manner that complies with the MPEG-2 standard for encoding video information for packaged media is expressly prohibited without a license under applicable patents in the MPEG-2 patent portfolio, which license is available from MPEG LA, L.L.C., 250 Steele Street, Suite 300 , Denver Colorado 80206

13. MISCELLANEOUS

13.1 This Agreement shall be governed by and interpreted in accordance with English law and not by the 1980 U. N. Convention on Contracts for the International Sale of Goods. If this License Agreement has been translated into a language which is not English and a dispute arises as to the meaning/ translation of any term of this License Agreement, the interpretation of the English version shall prevail. The parties agree to submit to the exclusive jurisdiction of the English Courts.

13.2 Except to the extent of any misrepresentation or breach of warranty which constitutes fraud and except in the case of a multi-user license agreement, this License Agreement constitutes the entire agreement between Serif and Licensee and supersedes all prior agreements, understandings, communications, advertising, proposals or representations, oral or written, by either party.

13.3 If any provision of this License Agreement is held invalid, illegal or unenforceable by a court of competent jurisdiction, such provision shall be severed and if possible revised to the extent necessary to cure the invalidity, illegality or non-enforceability, and the remainder of this License Agreement shall continue in full force and effect.

13.4 Any change to this License Agreement shall only be valid if it is in writing and signed by an authorized representative of both Serif and Licensee.

13.5 No failure, delay, relaxation or forbearance on the part of either party in exercising any power or right under this License Agreement shall operate as a waiver of such power or right or of any other power or right.

13.6 This License Agreement and the license granted pursuant to this License Agreement are personal to Licensee and except where permitted above Licensee shall not assign the benefit of or any interest or obligation under this License Agreement.

13.7 Apart from Serif's licensors and authorised distributors, a person who is not a party to this License Agreement has no right under the Contracts (Rights of Third Parties) Act 1999 or otherwise to enforce any term of this License Agreement. The consent of any third party is not required for any variation (including any release or compromise of any liability under this License Agreement) or termination of this License Agreement.

13.8 Further licenses relating to open source materials used in this product can be viewed in the licenses.rtf file included in this product

Berry Pie

Berry

Pie

1 2 3 !?&

abc ABC

Brushes

Frames

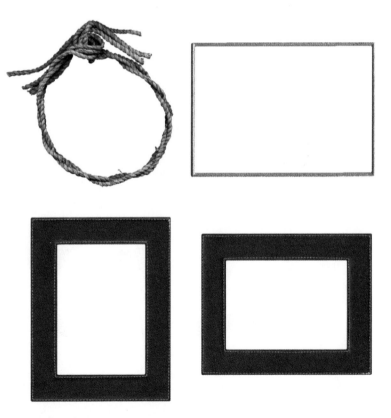

Embellishments

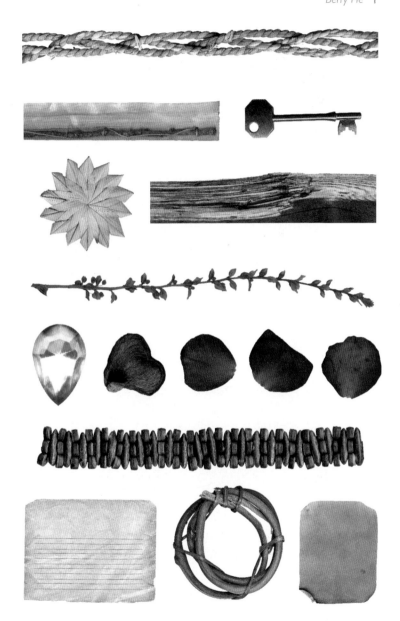

Sample Layouts

Materials

Backgrounds

Commando

COMMANDO

123!?&

ABCDEF

Brushes

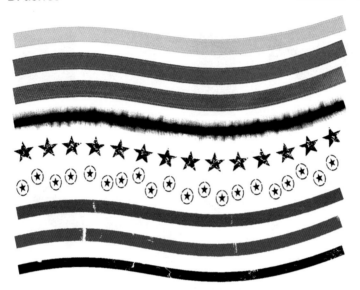

Frames

Embellishments

Sample Layouts

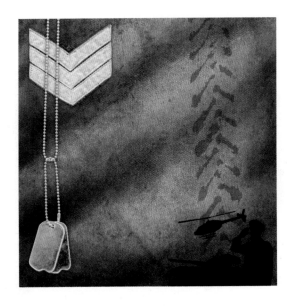

Materials

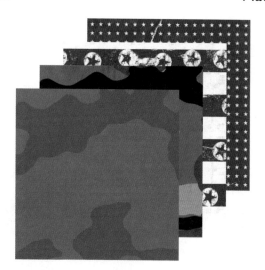

Backgrounds

Euro Tourist

Euro

Tourist

123!?&

abcABC

Brushes

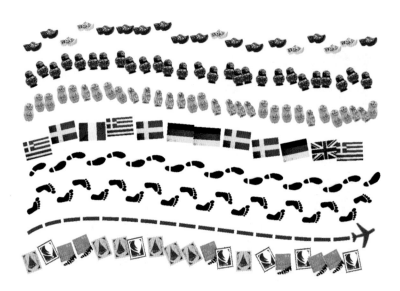

Frames

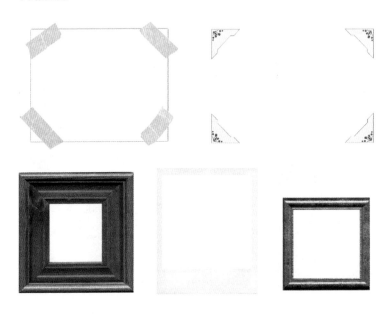

Embellishments

Materials

Backgrounds

Forbidden City

Forbidden

City

1 2 3 ! ? &

a b c A B C

Brushes

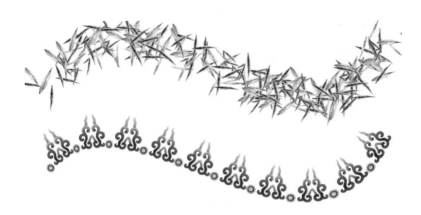

Frames

Embellishments

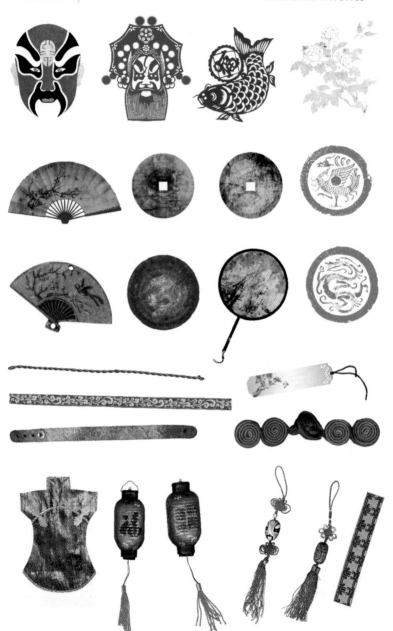

Rhythm

Buddhist

Wind

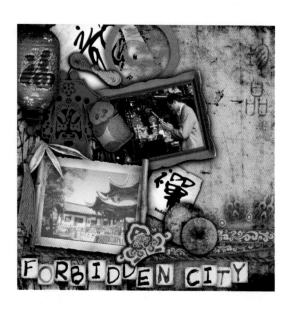

Materials

Backgrounds

Indie Chic

Brushes

Frames

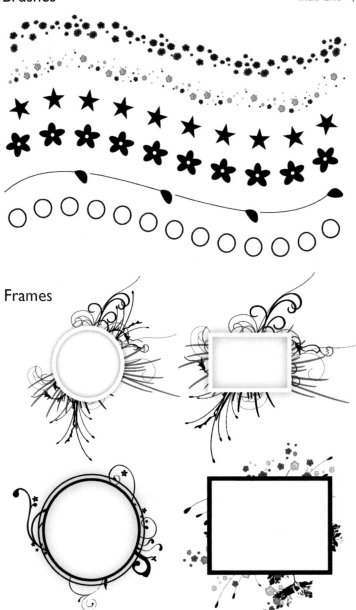

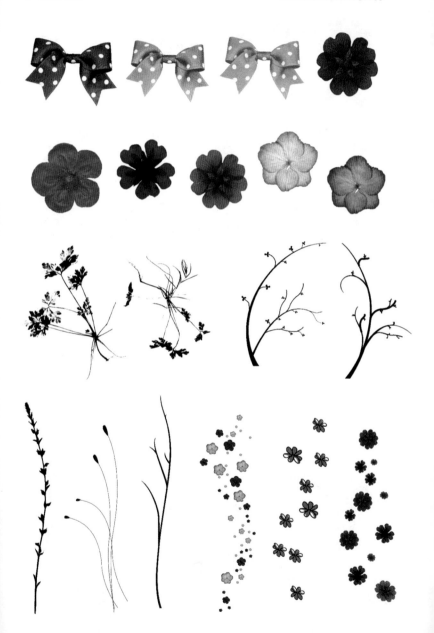

Sample Layouts

Materials

Backgrounds

Name That Tune

Brushes

Frames

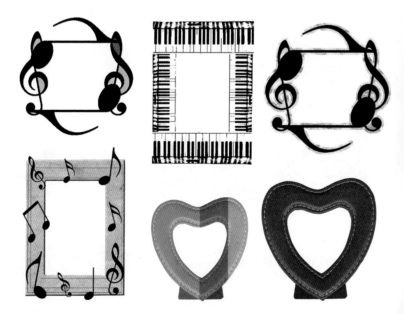

Embellishments

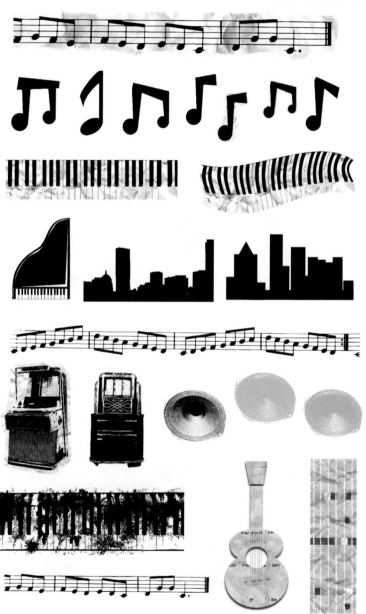

Materials

Backgrounds

Painted Backyard

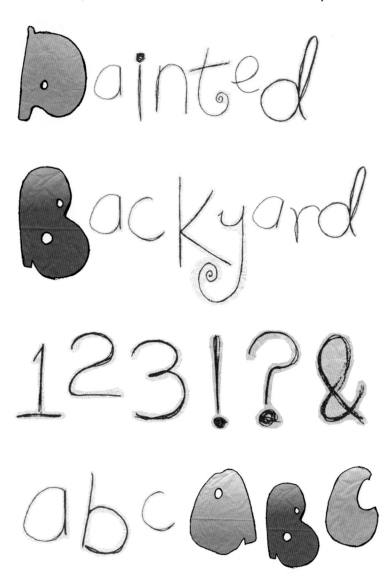

Brushes

Frames

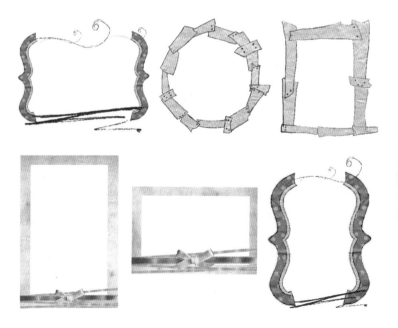

Embellishments

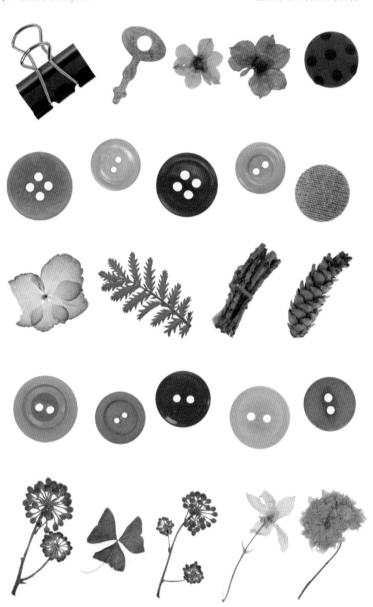

Sample Layouts

Materials

Backgrounds

Psychedelic

Psychedelic

1 2³ ! ? &

a b c A B C

Brushes

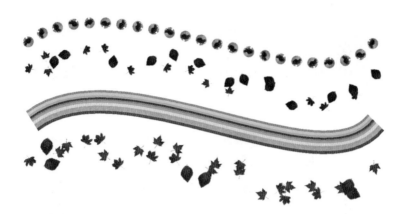

Frames

Embellishments

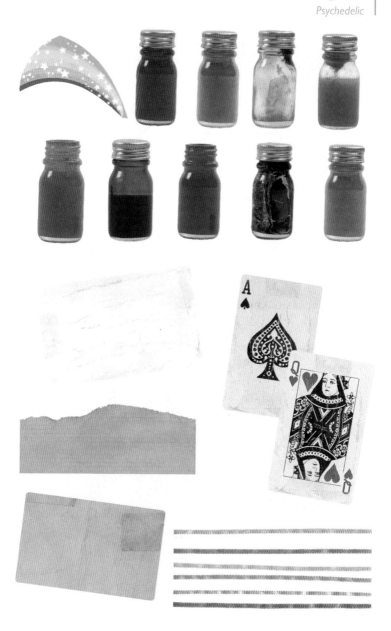

Sample Layouts

Materials

Backgrounds

Secret Garden

Alphabet

Brushes

Frames

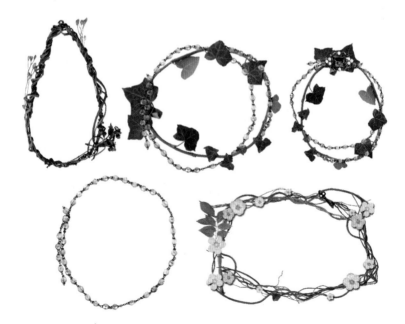

Embellishments

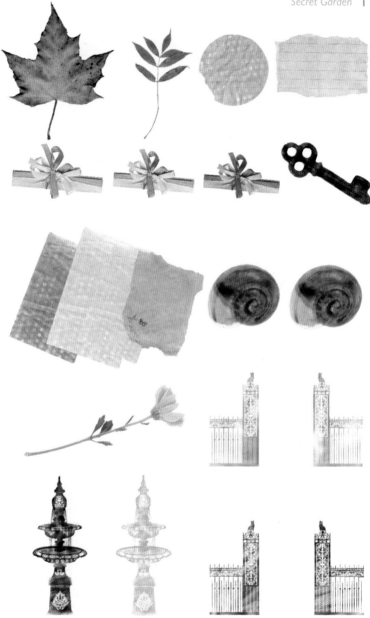

Sample Layouts

Materials

Backgrounds

Sweet Dreams

Sweet Dreams

1 2 3 ! ? &

a b c A B C

Brushes

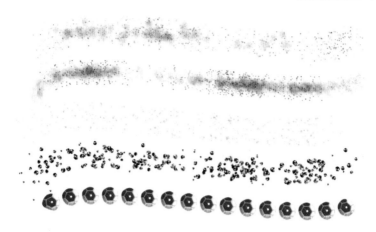

Frames

Embellishments

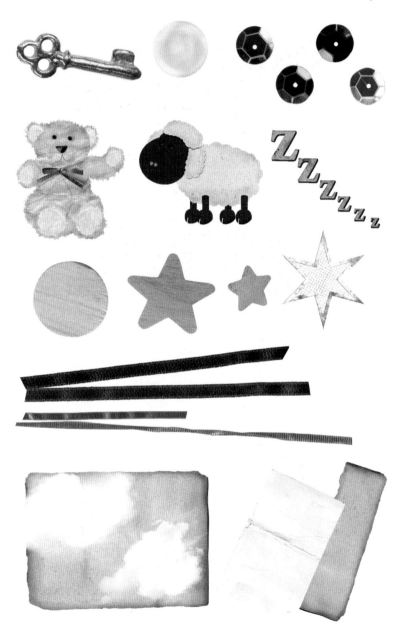

Sample Layouts

Materials

Backgrounds